11

For Eliot and Adam Benzecrit
R.A.

Text copyright © 1998 Roy Apps
Illustrations copyright © 1998 Sam Thompson

The right of Roy Apps to be identified as the author
of this work and the right of Sam Thompson to be
identified as the illustrator of this work has been
asserted to them in accordance with the Copyright,
Designs and Patents Act 1988.

This edition first published in Great Britain in 1998
by Macdonald Young Books, an imprint of
Wayland Publishers Limited

Typeset in 16/24pt Goudy

Printed and bound in Belgium by Proost N.V.

Macdonald Young Books
61 Western Road
Hove
East Sussex BN3 1JD

Find Macdonald Young Books on the Internet
http://www.myb.co.uk

ISBN 0 7500 2111 X

Anne Frank
The Last Days of Freedom

Roy Apps

Illustrated by Sam Thompson

MACDONALD YOUNG BOOKS

Chronology of
Anne Frank – The last days of freedom

12 June, 1929 Anne Frank is born in Frankfurt, Germany.

1933 The Nazis, the National Socialist Party, come to power in Germany, led by Adolf Hitler. He believes the German people are Aryans and that the Aryan race is the best. All other races, but especially the Jews, are inferior.

1933 The Frank family move to Amsterdam, Holland, to escape Nazi persecution of Jews.

1939 The Second World War breaks out.

1940 Germany invades and occupies Holland.

1941–2 More and more anti-Jewish laws are passed: all Jews have to carry an identity card stamped "J"; Jews are no longer allowed to own businesses; Jews are no longer allowed to own bicycles; Jewish children can only attend Jewish schools; all Jews have to wear a yellow star.

Summer 1941 Anne and her older sister, Margot, attend the Jewish School in Amsterdam.

12 June, 1942 (her 13th birthday) Anne receives a diary.

29 June, 1942 It is announced that all Jews in Holland are to be deported to labour camps. Officially this is so that they can report for work but as most Jews know these camps are really prison or concentration camps. Police begin raiding homes in Holland.

5 July, 1942 Margot Frank receives a call-up notice from the SS (the secret state police of the Nazis) ordering her to report for deportation to Westerbork (a transit camp for Jews going to the concentration camps).

6 July, 1942 The Frank family goes into hiding in the Secret Annexe at number 263 Prinsengracht.

13 July, 1942 The Van Pels family (Van Daan in Anne's diary) join the Frank family in the Secret Annexe.

4 August, 1944 The Secret Annexe occupants are discovered.

March 1945 Anne dies in Bergen-Belsen concentration camp.

1. A Wet Morning in July

It is half past seven in the morning. The straight, grey roads of Amsterdam are shining with rain.

Hurrying office workers huddle under grey macs and hats. Everyone seems to be wearing a hat: everyone, that is, except the soldiers. For this is 1942. Amsterdam is under German occupation.

A young woman and a girl come down the steps from a block of flats. The woman's name is Miep Gies. She looks like a secretary going to work – which she is. The girl, whose name is Margot Frank, slings her school satchel over her shoulder. She gets onto her bike and rides off after Miep.

A couple look briefly at Margot. One mutters to the other, "She's taking a risk." His friend nods. They know Margot is Jewish, because she wears a large, bright yellow star on her mac. It is against the law for Jews to ride bikes.

Inside the flat she has just left, Margot's father, mother and younger sister Anne have just finished their breakfast.

"Leave the clearing away," says her father. He sounds tense.

"Is it time?" asks her mother nervously.

Mr Frank nods.

He and his wife each pick up a shopping bag that is loaded to the brim.

Anne picks up a school satchel. She bends down to stroke a cat sleeping in the armchair.

"Bye, Moortje. You are going to a good home with our neighbours, you know. You'll come back with us, when this is over."

Moortje stretches a leg, then curls up tightly and returns to sleep.

"Anne!" calls her mother, sharply. "Come along! We have a long walk ahead of us!"

The warm July rain pours down.

Workers on their way to offices and shops clamber about the trams, school children leap onto buses. Everyone wants to get out of the rain.

Anne and her parents would like to get out of the rain too. But they can't. They are Jews. It is against the law for Jews to ride on trams or buses.

Some of the passers-by glance at them, sympathetically. They shrug to themselves as if to say, "we're sorry, but what can we do? It's the Germans. It's the Nazis. It's the war. It's the law." Nobody seems to think it strange that the young Jewish girl is wearing a hat and a scarf – in the middle of July. Or if they do, they say nothing.

The Franks turn into Prinsengracht, a tree-lined street running alongside one of Amsterdam's many canals.

Mr Frank glances around, as if he is afraid that someone is watching them.

Anne's head is full of thoughts. She is trying to remember when it was that she first got an inkling that something secret was going on. She supposes that it must have been about a month ago. The day of her birthday party...

2. The Missing Blouse

"Great party, Anne!"

"See you at school!"

One by one, Anne's friends left the flat. It *had* been a great party, she agreed. The highlight had been a film her father had shown called *The Lighthouse Keeper*, which had starred Rin Tin Tin, a really clever dog, who against all the odds, managed to save the Keeper from drowning.

Anne and her friends all loved films, but it was now against the law for Jews to go to cinemas.

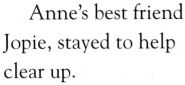

Anne's best friend Jopie, stayed to help clear up.

"What was your best present?" asked Jopie.

"My diary," replied Anne without hesitation.

"What are you going to write about in it?"

"Everything – and everybody."

"Even me?"

"Jopie, you are so vain," exclaimed Anne, laughing.

Anne gave her friend a nudge with her elbow. They were tidying away the cups. Anne's nudge made Jopie's hand slip and half a cup of somebody's left-over fizzy drink sloshed all down the front of her blouse.

"Drat!" exclaimed Jopie.

Anne tried not to giggle. "Sorry. You can't go home all dripping and sticky, Jopie, you'd better borrow one of my blouses."

She went across the hall to her bedroom and opened a drawer in her wardrobe.

There were no blouses there.

"But I'm sure there were *two* in there, when I got dressed this morning," she muttered to herself.

She was about to call her mother to ask what on earth was going on, but then something inside her – she knew not what – seemed to tell her not to.

So Jopie went home dripping and sticky.

Anne soon forgot about the missing blouse. It wasn't difficult. She had something else to think about and to write about in her diary.

"… he came shyly towards me and introduced himself as Harry Goldberg."

3. Harry's Story

She had left the flat that morning and on her way past the bike racks, Harry Goldberg had leapt out and asked her, bold as brass, "Hi, would you like to walk to school with me?"

"As you're going my way in any case, I will," Anne shrugged, as if it was all of no consequence, but her heart was thumping.

Harry and Anne went to the Jewish School: it was against the law for Jewish children to go anywhere other than special Jewish schools.

Everyone at the Jewish School was awaiting the exam results. Wim and Jacques, who sat behind Anne in class, were even taking bets about who would move up a class.

"What about Anne?"

"Must be a dead cert."

Anne turned round. "Will you two stop talking about me as if I'm a racehorse," she said in a cross voice. Though really she was rather pleased that the boys thought she was clever enough to go up a class.

"Anne Frank, face the front!" said Mr Keptor. "You're nothing but a chatterbox! I've a mind to –"

But whether it was a detention or extra homework Mr Keptor had in mind, Anne never found out, because the bell went for end of school.

Harry was waiting for her at the gate.

Over the next few days, Anne saw a lot of Harry. She liked him. He was tall and good-looking – and he told good jokes.

One warm summer's evening a week later, they were leaning on the railing overlooking the canal.

"I don't know about you, but I could do with an ice cream," said Harry.

"There isn't anywhere," sighed Anne.

Their eyes scanned the rows of cafes and ice cream shops. In the front window of every one was a large sign:

VOOR JODEN VERBODEN

Forbidden to Jews.

Harry's face darkened. "Voor Joden Verboden! We're not animals!"

"The Nazis think we are," said Anne, trying somehow to make light of it; desperate not to have her evening spoiled. "When the war is over and the Nazis are no more, then you can buy me an ice cream, Harry."

Harry leant further over the railings. He was looking down, deep into the canal.

"Are your parents making plans, Anne?"

"Plans…?" Anne shivered, though she didn't know why.

"Yes…" Harry saw Anne's puzzled and worried face. "It's nothing," he shrugged. "Come on, I'd better be getting you home."

Anne's father was at the door. His face was red with anger.

"Do you know what the time is?"

"It's only ten past eight –"

"It's dangerous for Jews to be out on the streets so late!"

"I'm sorry, Mr Frank," said Harry. "It was my fault."

Mr Frank softened his tone a little. "Yes, well, don't let it happen again. And young man, take care walking home."

Anne lay in bed, her mind buzzing with thoughts about Harry. What were the "plans" he had mentioned? Why had her father lost his temper like that? He had been a bit fed up, she knew, ever since he'd had to sell his firm: it was against the law for Jews to own businesses.

Anne felt hungry. She got up and tiptoed through to the kitchen.

She opened the larder door. There was a new packet of biscuits in there, she knew. She had seen them at tea time. Her eyes scanned the shelves: no biscuits. Surely Margot hadn't scoffed the lot?

In fact, the whole larder looked decidedly more empty than it had at tea time.

All of a sudden, Anne remembered the missing blouse.

She wandered back to her bed, hungry, wide awake and anxious.

27

Lying in bed, Anne made up her mind. Tomorrow, she would pick her moment and ask her mother and father just what was going on. She was sure Margot knew something; well then, why shouldn't she? She was thirteen years old, after all.

4. The Secret Plan

Anne and her father walked across the little square that fronted their block of flats. Bright red and yellow roses blossomed in the warm summer's sunshine.

This, Anne decided, would be the moment she would ask just what was going on.

"Are you and mum pleased with my exam results?"

Mr Frank nodded. He had a faraway look.

"I'm really looking forward to moving up a class next term."

Mr Frank nodded again.

"I feel quite grown up already. Still, I am *thirteen*…" said Anne pointedly.

Another distant nod from Mr Frank.

"What I mean is that I'm old enough to be told things – like Margot!"

It hadn't come out quite how Anne had meant it to. Her father stopped.

"Yes Anne. You must be told."

He sat down on the grass and Anne
joined him.

"It is only a matter of time before the
German authorities call up all Jews."

"Call them up where?"

"To concentration camps – or work
camps as they like to call them – in
Germany. I don't intend it to happen to me.
That's why we've been taking food and
clothes from the flat. Ready for us all to go
into hiding."

"Where?" asked Anne. Mr Frank shook his head. "I can't tell you that, Anne." He spoke so seriously, that Anne's voice trembled with anxiety as she struggled to understand the enormity of what he was saying.

"When?" she whispered.

"Who knows? Probably a long way off yet. Make the most of your life while you can."

And with those words, Mr Frank got up and strode back to the flat. Anne followed.

Never before had the yellow star seemed to weigh so heavily on her dress.

A long way off yet… Make it a very long way off, she thought to herself as she wrote her diary that night. Make it a very long way off indeed.

5. The World Turned Upside Down

The next Sunday, Anne was lying on the balcony reading a book in the sunshine. She was waiting for Harry.

She looked at her watch. He was late.

She went through to the kitchen. Margot
was standing there, looking flushed and
excited.

"Didn't you hear the door bell?"

Anne shook her head.

"Was it Harry? Where is he?"

"It wasn't Harry," said Margot. "It was a
call-up notice from the SS."

"They haven't taken dad away, have
they?" asked Anne, frantically.

"No. No. He's still out visiting some elderly ladies in the old people's home."

Anne breathed a sigh of relief.

"He's not going to any camp!" declared Margot.

"We have to go into hiding – already?" asked Anne.

"Yes," said Margot. "Mum's gone to warn the Van Daans. They will be coming with us."

Suddenly the door bell rang again.

Anne rushed to the kitchen door, but Margot dragged her back.

"But that could be Harry!" protested Anne.

"Sshhhh!"

The two girls stood perfectly, silently still.

They heard the door open.

They heard their mother's voice, then Mr Van Daan's. Then they heard Harry's voice. Anne made to move to the kitchen door, but Margot's strong grip held her fast.

"No Anne! It's better you stay here."

Mrs Frank and Mrs Van Daan came in to the kitchen.

"Where's Harry?" asked Anne.

"Leave us girls, will you," said Mrs Frank. "Mrs Van Daan and I need to talk alone.

In the quiet of their bedroom, Margot took her younger sister's hand in hers.

"Anne," she said, "I wasn't quite truthful with you about the call-up." She paused. "It wasn't daddy they sent for, it was me."

Anne gulped. "But you're only *sixteen!*"

"Oh, I'm not going to any concentration camp," said Margot, breezily. "I'm going into hiding with you and mum and dad and the Van Daans."

Anne burst into tears.

It was some time before she could stop.

"Harry…" she murmured. "He's sixteen, too."

"I'm sure he's got arrangements," said Margot, gently.

6. The Secret Annexe

…And so it is that one wet morning in July, Anne, her mother and father turn into Prinsengracht, a tree-lined street running alongside a canal.

Mr Frank glances around, as if he is afraid that someone is watching them.

But the soldiers on the corner are too busy chatting to a couple of girls.

"Hurry! Hurry!" he whispers, quickly ushering Anne and her mother into a handsome block of houses. Suddenly, Anne realises it's her father's old office. He slams the door behind him and locks it fast.

Waiting inside is Miep, the young woman Margot had left the flat with. Her eyes are wide and urgent.

"Quickly!" she instructs the family.

They make their way up the creaking stairs. At the top is a huge bookcase. Anne frowns at the row of books; trying to read some of the titles.

"There is no time for that, Anne!" scolds her mother.

"Help us push," says Miep.

"Push?" asks Anne, puzzled.

Then she sees Miep and her father and mother all pushing the bookcase along. She pushes it too, all of a sudden it opens to reveal a door: a door to a secret room.

And there is Margot.

"Mummy! Daddy! Anne!"

"I must go!" says Miep.

The Franks shut the secret bookcase door behind her.

While Margot hugs her parents, Anne stands perfectly still. Only now has it dawned on her that her days of freedom are over. From now on, there will be no more chats with Jopie, no more ice creams with Harry, no going up a class next term. At once she feels both terrified and excited. Her life in hiding has begun.

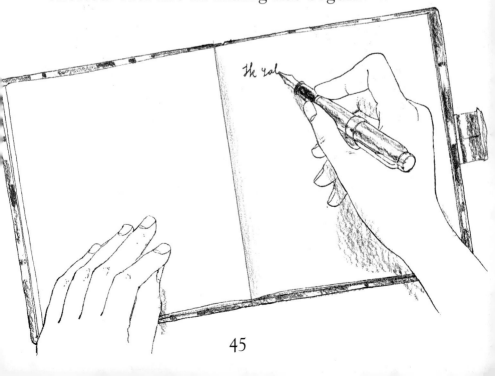

The Diary of Anne Frank

For just over two years, Anne Frank kept a diary of her life in the secret annexe. Then on August 4, 1944, she and the others were betrayed and arrested by German Security Police, accompanied by Dutch Nazis.

Anne died in Bergen-Belsen Concentration Camp in March 1945, a few weeks before the camp was liberated by the British Army. She was one of six million Jews murdered by the Nazis.

Anne's diary was left behind by the Nazis, when she was arrested. Miep Gies kept it. After the war, Anne's father, the only member of the family not to die in the camps, arranged for it to be published.

Since then, **The Diary of Anne Frank** has been published in fifty-five languages.